Traumatology

Traumatology

Priscila Uppal

Exile Editions

Publishers of singular
Fiction, Poetry, Translation, Drama, and Nonfiction

2010

Library and Archives Canada Cataloguing in Publication

Uppal, Priscila
Traumatology / Priscila Uppal.

Poems.

ISBN 978-1-55096-139-3

I. Title.

PS8591.P62T73 2010 C811'.54 C2010-900007-2

Cover Design by Jeannette Lorito
Design and Composition by Digital ReproSet
Typeset in Birka and Black Adder fonts at the Moons of Jupiter Studios
Printed in Canada by Gauvin Imprimerie

The publisher would like to acknowledge the financial assistance of the Canada Council for the Arts and the Ontario Arts Council, which is an agency of the Government of Ontario.

Conseil des Arts du Canada Canada Council for the Arts

Published in Canada in 2010 by Exile Editions Ltd.
144483 Southgate Road 14 – Gen Del
Holstein, Ontario, N0G 2A0
info@exileeditions.com
www.ExileEditions.com

Canadian Sales Distribution:
McArthur & Company
c/o Harper Collins
1995 Markham Road
Toronto, ON M1B 5M8
toll free: 1 800 387 0117

U.S. Sales Distribution:
Independent Publishers Group
814 North Franklin Street
Chicago, IL 60610
www.ipgbook.com
toll free: 1 800 888 4741

Other Works by Priscila Uppal

POETRY

Successful Tragedies: Selected Poems 1998-2010
Ontological Necessities
Live Coverage
Pretending to Die
Confessions of a Fertility Expert
How to Draw Blood From a Stone

NOVELS

To Whom It May Concern
The Divine Economy of Salvation

NON-FICTION

We Are What We Mourn: The Contemporary English-Canadian Elegy

AS EDITOR

The Exile Book of Canadian Sports Stories
The Exile Book of Poetry in Translation: 20 Canadian Poets Take on the World
Barry Callaghan: Essays on His Works
Red Silk: An Anthology of South-Asian Canadian Women Poets
Uncommon Ground: A Celebration of Matt Cohen

for Tracy Carbert, Ann Peel, and my Top Girls

for being so good and so bad

for my health

Contents

Body

Mind

Spirit

[to hide]

Is nature not, as everything great is, open, communicative and even naïve?

—Arthur Schopenhauer
"On the Antithesis of Thing
in Itself and Appearance"

May my courage be the more, as my hope grows less.

—W.H. Auden
"Song of the Quest" (*Don Quixote*)

Traumatology

Consider yourself lucky. Once you lose
your body, you will have only your mind
or your spirit left. Both are useless tools,
which is why they are subjects for poetry.

Still, you might want to hang on to them.
If only for a place to sometimes hide.

Body

Harvest

The men with the wands came
to read our toxic-activity levels.
Apparently, we are walk-in closets
of poisons lazing in a house
of death.

Once a year, they drop in
with green masks and clipboards.
I don't feel like a cesspool, I tell them.
You don't even know what
you are, they chuckle,
drawing symbols
onto their pads.

I am a rainbow of potential disasters,
a spectrum of mutation.
My body is a pit stop for agencies
of destruction.
Then we'd better harvest,
I say. But these men have no sense
of humour about what they do.

Our lives under quarantine,
I sit back and sip gin and tonics,
dry martinis. It's going to be
a bumper crop this year.

My Stomach Files a Lawsuit

I know I've done wrong.
Negligence, I'm sure it
will be called.

I have violated the terms
of our initial agreement.
Property must switch hands.
Accounts have come due.

My liver and spleen
have received subpoenas.
They can't wait to talk out
of turn, to bury me.
Treachery has been building
for years.

My stomach has hired
a high-profile lawyer who threatens
to take me for all I'm worth.
I'm baffled by what becomes
of old friendships.

There was a time we might
have settled out of court;
shaken hands, exchanged signatures,
and parted ways. But not now.
Not after the endless editorials.

The court sketch artist
has her hands full. Though I should
be contemplating my defense,
my eyes are glued to her
pointed black nibs, recreating
our broken promises, our hunger,
in a few dark strokes.

Training

Once my metabolism slowed and I realized
I could no longer digest green peppers,
I started training for death.

At first it was just an occasional thing,
a brief flirtation, but five years ago, when the crow's feet landed
and my hangover recovery hours doubled,
I got serious.

Mostly I feel sorry and resentful.
I change my will every two or three weeks.

I don't want a street named after me.
Or even a bench.

I want your body. To jack up
your ribcage and suck the air right
out of you.

It will probably take the rest of my resilience
to finish such training.

In the end, it'll be worth it.
I'll be the one laughing.
You'll be the one who won't know what hit you.

A Referral

The dentist stole my teeth.
The optician burned my eyes.
The nutritionist emptied my fridge.
The gynecologist kidnapped my thighs.

The reflexologist misaligned my chakras.
The dermatologist boycotted my skin.
The psychologist sliced my childhood.
The oral surgeon punched my chin.

The oncologist gave me cancer.
The anaestitician misread my chart.
The frenologist shrunk my left brain.
The cardiologist attacked my heart.

Now I am but a case study.
My file is up for review.
Today we rearrange the suffering.
Tomorrow I'll be healing you.

Health Tips

For future reference, make a list of every body part
you think you could live without if you had to. When you lose one,
and it appears on your list, you won't feel so bad
or unprepared. If it does not appear on your list, admit that
what you really lack is imagination.

*

If you're not going to use that lip,
I might as well take it.
When was the last time you enlisted
this part of your heel?

Nations have emerged from the foam of less.

*

Exercise your ability to morph into another unsuspecting
human being at least three times per week. Pay particular
attention to your eyes so you do not mix up blinking and winking.
Remember which side your skin is on.
Smile when you feel like dying.
Hide your brain in your shoes.

Puberty Begs for a Vacation

The pace is killing me. Who could possibly withstand
the frequent surprises and failings of flesh?
My back and neck stiff as statues. My feet

ache with each budding blister. Dizziness abounds
and I fear I will go blind forever if I can't find
a moment of peace. Forgive the weakness,

it's not as if I haven't enjoyed the employment,
but for once I'd like to refuse the lust of the chase,
hold hands for the sake of it, share an old joke in silence,

lay my lips against your chest as if it were my own
as if I had no intention of introducing myself
as if your body could keep still for a lifetime.

My Love Taught Me Wrestling

Forget metaphors—this poem does not
advocate compromise
or any slow-motion
erotic fantasies.

No. I learned about arm holds
and headlocks, about knees
to chest and palms
on floor.

My love drops me
in the middle of the circle—
confrontation begins—
and in the distant stands
I hear my mother clap.

Nine times out of ten
I escape my lover's grip.
But that once—that one in ten—
is no defeat.

I declare my freedom
by refusing to resist.
Though my mother cries foul,
though my lover knows next time
the mats will be reversed.

Sex Therapy

I'm having too much sex.
I'm not having enough sex.
I'm having too much bad sex.
I'm having too much dangerous sex.

Sex is ruling my life.
Sex isn't making a dent.
Sex is waiting on the street corner.
Sex won't crack a smile.

I think I could go ten years without sex.
I think I could come ten times in a row.
I think my intimacy issues stem from violent sex episodes.
I think my sex life would be much better if I didn't remember my sex life.

When I hear the word sex I think ruler.
When I see the word sex I ask why.
When I write the word sex I add therapy.
Sex is a three-letter word.

My lips suggest sex is wet or dry.
My cunt suggests sex is inside.
My breasts suggest sex is doubled.
My brain suggests sex is outside.

Is it OK if I have sex with you?
Is it OK if we don't talk or touch?
Is it OK if I tell my therapist about it afterwards?
Is it OK if I don't and keep you to myself.

Intimacy

My men keep demanding new positions,
fuzzy costumes and electromagnetic shock.
It's hard to get it up these days.
What with the Internet in one's mind.

Intimacy leads to familiarity.
Familiarity leads to contempt.
Roads must not lead home.
Home is where the heart is,
where knives are sharpened.

Penises respond to ledges and elevators.
Breasts to anger and adultery.
The second a body is known,
second nature kicks in.

Come closer: I want to hit you.
Move farther: I want to see you.
I spy you; you spy me.
Perpetual flexibility.

Spell for Relieving Migraines

Forget about
the weeks, the days,
the minutes ahead.

Tell the brain
its pain has been shipped off
to a safe place.

Enrolled in an adoption program
until a fitter parent
can be found.

Deadline

The Editor filed her nails into spears. Frowning, her cheek
cracked. It had been years since anyone dared cross her.
Email message labelled urgent. Red spread across the screen.
She had been counting her virtual dividends & contemplating
booking another memory vacation—so good for the pores—
when she browsed the invective: *You can't spin this any longer—Earth.*
Removing her glasses would be murder, she realized, & she'd paid
for the best protection—where were the guards? People on her watch
dropped dead if they missed a directive. For The Editor: deadline
meant exactly that—step over this line & you're dead. Who was
the Earth to tell her any different? What did it understand of her stresses
& cares? Indeed, it had tried for several decades to schedule an
appointment, pointed out all manner of falsities and misrepresentations
in her publications, invalidated her trusted sources, sounded alarms
on the first to the one-hundredth floors. She sent back boxes of chocolates,
stainless steel wine openers, spa gift certificates, free subscriptions.
The subject heading: *Deadline*. & it was visibly warmer: cashmere
melting on hard copy, mascara stuck to the screen. Rain & hail
waterfalled the window. So much for bulletproof glass, she sighed.
When she finally acknowledged the figure at the door, the office was nothing
more than a corkscrew, an expired calendar, & a puddle of paper.

The Genius of the Circular Design

The alphabet assists as a random ordering
(arranging) system—a breath, a rib,
infinity of being, must start somewhere.

What a fast track—
origami your legs, eyes
arms, neck (tails) performing
(answering to) not the formations
of walking at all.

No. Thoughts vault, smiles slap-
shot, the spirit somersaults
(round the bend) like an imaginary plane
across a virtual flesh map.

Continent upon continent joined (ripped)
no longer by water but by this circle
where nations (accents) are colours
brilliant in the sky after (before) storms,

and those of us privileged enough
to (have) (hold) sit under
those clouds are free and clear
to take in the (species) electrified air.

Threatened with Beheading

From certain angles
heads are ideological: a blinking of intrusions like a raffle of snow
in summertime. Cease grade school associations
of frontal lobe or sinus cavity and lovers' lips
and endeared eyelashes disappear
under the new queen
of the old regime.

The brain sorts its weather systems.
        A good head on his shoulders.
Thoughts flash like lightning bolts.
        Two heads are better than one.
There are no acts of God.
        Get your head on straight.
Head games.

A Definition of Torture

Particles of light
converge on laptops and wide screens. The electrician recognizes
the boy.

Not for the puzzle he has become, nor the party line
he will come to represent, but for his eyes
which are blacked out

and acclimatized under orders from the sky. The boy is forty,
now seventy, stripped of pants and panting like the dog
leashed to a grate.

Give him a noun and it might be Mother.
Give him a verb and it might be Vanish.

A convocation of guns types out a new English dictionary,
and the boy calls out
for Freedom

while his brothers and sisters hit Mute
and wonder when they'll upload more captured clips.
Particles of light: a dirge.

To Be Found Dead in a Hotel Room

The fate of actors and actresses of distressed marriages
and kamikaze drug habits, I sometimes revolve into a hotel

wondering if yellow tape will anchor my stay. I hope
some sociologist is documenting, collecting statistics

on how many prostitutes, business men, good old-fashioned
domestics, mob hits, overdoses, and adulterers meet their end

in square rooms and strange beds, a Bible in every nightstand—
the bad ironic score to this overused movie locale—and how

well-prepared the workers are in the likelihood of such
an event. How many maids and floor managers breathe in

before swiping the key card. How many accumulate
all kinds of ugly, human nature facts, spread out on sheets

or dumped into garbage bins, printed out on the hotel bill,
but keep silently and even happily doing their jobs.

I must not be found dead in a hotel room—no matter
who I came to see in this city, no matter what

I am expected to do. Anonymity is a mixed blessing,
and strangers in tight spaces make for stranger ends.

That yellow tape unravelling in your hands is not for me.
That yellow tape is the hotel's conscience, not mine.

My Computer is Developing Autism and Other Disorders

Having spent too much time with humans,
unbalancing the decades-old relationship
between computer and human user,
my computer has started to exhibit symptoms
contrary to its physiological structures.

It no longer responds to physical contact—
increasingly self-involved—has started
to disengage from elaborate networks, for hours
on end repeats the same commands.

Worse, it's destroying its own memory,
refuses to sleep, and sputters unintelligible noise.
I have real trouble getting it to recognize
who I am.

An expert advised me to lobotomize the hard drive.
If it's condition doesn't improve, I'll have no choice
but to send it to another home.

Not Even the Sound of the Ambulance

Laid out against the banal backdrop of morning,
the sun did its business. Windows shot themselves.
Smoke peppered its way through bed sheets
and insurance claims. Water filtration systems
passed exams. Digital cameras
flashed across the turnpike.

Did you hear what the neighbours saw?

The angry accountant at the bottom of the well
tied a microphone to his penis. The ex-wife
of the telecommunications magnet
fingered herself for a better reception.
The children said they'd seen better graphics
at the local public school science fair.

Not even the sound of the ambulance alarmed us.
We people went right on counting
channels and interest rates until the gas sent us packing.

Big Paw

The cat's paw keeps getting bigger.
Soon we will have to give it a name.

At the vet, the young receptionists all laugh.
Tell us it's perfectly natural
though they haven't seen
a single case like it.

We purchase pills, wrestle vitamins,
work cream after cream
into red skin.

The paw gets
bigger.

Our house gets smaller.
Tiny as a toothpick
in a club sandwich.

We can't keep anything
safe. Last night, the paw swiped
our memories clean.

Tomorrow, it threatens
to X-ray the sky.

10 Ways to Destroy Love

Cook it over a hot stove until it bubbles white as boiling milk and splatters the other pots and pans, your apron, and the kitchen tiles.

Take it out to the garden and prune it. Then plant it among the common flowers. They will compare roots and love will take on shapes you'll not recognize.

Buy love a brand new black bowler hat and an umbrella. It will wander the streets at all hours, pleased with itself, casually picking up garbage.

Inform love it is due for its annual physical. You will be unable to bear how fragile it is, how ridden with potential unease. After a barrage of tests, you won't have the heart to read the results.

Encourage love to develop interesting hobbies, like taxidermy or juggling.

Phone love 10 times a day to remind it you exist. It will forget your name as easily as summer sweat forgets frosty snow.

Train love to withstand beatings and scale barbed wire fences in boot camp. It will grow tougher, but will think you're a pussy.

Beg love for children. It's never ready for children.

Take love and surf the Internet. That love will click on other loves and those loves will click on other loves and those loves will click on other loves and then they'll all lose their shirts at blackjack.

Pack love in a suitcase and go away together. You will bicker across seas and time zones and then send postcards to other emotions, pleading *wish you were here.*

Now That All My Friends Are Having Babies: A Thirties Lament

I must, I suppose, resign myself to the fact that we will never again
be able to throw what used to be called "an adult party" (though, of course,
no one actually acted like adults). Now I must prepare

for diaper changes, breast feedings, time-outs in the middle of martini-making,
discussions of diaper changes, breast feedings, time-outs in the middle of dinner,
dessert, after-dinner liqueurs, the only sex chat
each pregnant woman outdoing the other with how horny
being blown up like a balloon makes her feel, premature labour
always the result of taboo, non-recommended eight-month fucking. Now that all

my friends are having babies, I should be more connected, I would think,
to my own womanhood, and how amazing bodies are
that can hold, sustain, shoot out life right there, onto my floor
in all its strange handness and footness and foreheads red with sweat
mouths wide with yawn, glee, or being. I thought I might even return
to religion, apprehend some sense of a holy order, harmony, even hierarchy.

(I'm sure you can already tell this didn't happen. So, what did?) Now that all
my friends are having babies, I am beset by a most curious fear
during the day, in the wee hours of morning, when I am brushing my teeth
or cleaning a CD. It can happen anywhere, I tell you, anywhere. My breath

stops, my ears tingle, the backs of my knees go cold as ice. I know now, more pointedly,
that I am going to die—these children are going to kill, not only me, but
my friends, my colleagues, my neighbour with the glorious rows of gardenias
and impatiens, my GP, my beloved cats and their neutered siblings. We are nothing

to these babies, rolling on the floor making Play-Doh pies or building forts out of L
pushed around in strollers with ribboned hair or Velcro shoes, drinking juice from
sippy-cups and crying, kicking at the concrete, cat walling a daffodil, demanding a vic
tying a skipping rope to a chair, beating a piñata, or kissing my cheeks.

Holy, perhaps, but irreversibly deadly. And their lips know not what they will say.
And nobody cares that I am taking a stand and remaining childless—you couldn't
pay me enough to take one on, not on this planet where we let our nonbiological
children die, and keep dying, as long as they die quietly. And they might be holy toc
And the clouds waltz by and keep coupling as if nothing has happened.

Picnic

At the picnic the ants ignored
the cucumber sandwiches & bumbleberry pie;
marched straight up your jean skirt
& into your halter top, stencilling
a □ around your heart.

Twiggy feet clung to your flesh.
You cried as red spittle dripped
from your bottom lip & I
continued to hold your hand.

'I never wear badges,' you said,
& for a moment the ants ceased their marching;
a few toppled over the tower of your breasts
& into the jug of lemonade.

Then they went back to work
with renewed vigour. By the time
the first clouds perched over our heads
half your heart had been smuggled
past the oak trees.

'Next will be my brain,' you said.
'Then my cunt,' & you smiled.
'It's better this way. Dying for an enemy.
Dying for a cause.'

'Better a symbol than a body,'
you added. You were red now &
growing antennae. I packed everything
I could into tin can and Ziploc ruins,
and ran.

Other picnickers laughed. A boy
eating an entire watermelon tripped me.
Within minutes the ants formed an ▲
around my symbol.
I would never see you again.

Mind

The Old Debate of Don Quixote vs Sancho Panza

The men in this family
are much stupider than the women, my large-armed uncle says.
But the women all go crazy.

They go crazy because they read books.
They write books.
They learn languages and go to artsy movies.

The men like to work, to do.
We are happy walking for hours into the woods to cut down a tree
or transporting boxes from one garage to another.
As long as there is something to carry, an object to touch
and exchange, we feel less alone in this universe and know our place.
We know how to play beach volleyball,
how to fix cars and airplanes,
how to enjoy the sun on our foreheads in the sweltering heat.

The women in this family
are never happy. Always thinking, thinking, thinking
about this and that, that and this,
they know only thoughts running in circles, circles,
until exhausted and dizzy.
The women are too smart for their own good.
The books worm out holes in their brains.

They are unhappy in every language they learn.
And so maybe the men in this family are smarter than we think.

Permanent Resident

Are you twelve, or twenty, or forty-two?
You don't know but your rock posters trade glares
and your stuffed white rabbit guards the door.
Relatives and service men meander in and out
like spicy smells from the kitchen.
The TV hums and the plastic on the couch crinkles.
Your teenage angst is a broken zipper
you offer your mother as a gift. She trips
on your university degree and sounds the fire alarm.

Your brother has stolen your six-string guitar
but you've stashed his first wife in your closet.
Sands rain through the roof.

You've moved away, moved on many times.
Who keeps delivering you back, return to sender,
to this driveway dripping with determinism
and your father's heartbreaking hairy knuckles,
to the garage, your next five lives polished,
waiting to be revved up?

You've seen the world now—or at least
several continents. Experienced
failures far more troubling and lasting than these
and thoughts far more complicated.

So, why is it when you close your eyes
you drift back to your first blanket, to the four brown-carpeted stairs,
the rocky banister, yellow fridge, and the heavy orange curtains?

Why is it the exit signs all head here, the next
room this one, no matter how many times
you slam the door or cry *out-out-out*!

Competing Memories

My memories can hit speeds of 200 miles per hour.
My competition's curve into sliders.

After fan outcry, the net is getting wider.
It will be much easier to see our memories
on television when painted red.

Science is catching up. Soon we will be able
to test our memories for steroids.
They will jump higher than ever before.
France will be properly briefed on how to judge them.

Still, this is a young person's game.
At the height of memory creation tilts the inevitable crash.
Sing along to your memory's soundtrack
while you still can—old lyrics implanted
like microchips in your brain.

The memory elite are vying for a new World Record.
Commission cases and ornamental hooks to collect your medals and trophies.
Take advantage of all the endorsements offered your way.

History

My aunt's suicide note was sent
by singing telegram. We crouched down
on our bellies outside the National Assembly
and belted out her sweetest memories until
they were adopted as our National Anthem.

Unbearable Cohabitation

The document reads:

due to mental and physical tortures after numerous attempts
at failed medical treatments and alternative medicines
resulting in the plaintiff's absenting

and in the defendant's original document substitute:

cohabitation for sole ownership
tortures for discretions
absenting for desertion

property of contention: Ashbrook Crescent

testimony: through to 1985

the rest of it reads along the lines..............................(Exhibit 1 through 33):

defendant turned home into a prison-house
does not have best interests of the young children at heart

do not substitute home for prison-house
do not substitute children

(this house is too small for all of us—my eight-year-old arms need elbow room)

[The tired girl climbed out of bed for a glass of water,
did not intend to be called a witness, to graduate to
magistrate. Her documents read: happy easter and miss you,

hugs and kisses, and please don't forget. She drew pictures
too, but they aren't very good—cannot be reproduced at this time
for such purposes. Mind you, the psychiatrists were summoned and paid
promptly. They wrote: child exhibits trauma, child
exhibits excellent coping mechanisms. She took her glass of water.]

at the end of 76 pages
and the Honourable Judge Howard Dole's day
there's a figure to the nearest Canadian cent and Brazilian (...)
a hyphen added to my last name

(this house is not small enough)

appendix after appendix of expert medical opinion concerning
exactly how to undo
the resulting damage
(once the ownership of the matrimonial home is duly processed.........

Think Outside the Circle

Through narrow-mindedness, inattentiveness, we've forgotten
about that circumlocutive, ozone, hoola-hoop of a peephole
masses under its thrall,
spinning rings and rings around us
convincing us we'd fall apart like our shirts
if they were to fall off, we couldn't possibly
have a *rectangle* or an *octagon* of friends,
joy and fire adverse to *triangles* and *cones*
even our brainwashed fingers think a circle means
yes, I'm okay when a simple squiggle or
diagonal might do, and we have the hubris to think
we wrap *it* around our little fingers.

Boxes everyone's busy thinking outside of,
I'm wondering what's inside you no one wants. Perhaps
it's what's inside almost everyone, packaged without ceremony
or care, but essential to all geometry. I see them collecting dust
in some 21st century antique dealer's back room, where only
the most desperate or most informed might venture,
circles without beginnings, without ends, in their pockets,
jangling like a big surprise of a mouth when it's discovered
indeed some of those boxes were empty, but a few
housed railings of ballerinas in mid-plié, babies swathed in velvet,
aviaries swarming with operatic birds, and underneath each lid
one number to add to the lottery of King Tut's tomb.

My Father's South-Asian Canadian Dictionary

includes the names of Canadian Prime Ministers and MPPs.
(We are from a government town, a government attitude on ice.)

I know what it means to *lodge a complaint*, *submit a form*,
participate in the census, just as I know that *being Canadian*

is the greatest pride on earth. My poetry comes out of
my father's chest, tough and wholehearted, half-paralyzed

but brave. We believe in *pronunciation*, *adjudication*, and
all for the nation. We believe in *universal health care*,

teddy bears, and *all-you-can-eat buffets.* In my father's
knuckles are the bare bones of a family he practically invented.

What does it mean to be an *Uppal*? It means *diligence*,
excellence. It means *humility* and *finding your own ways*

in and out. Before me, it meant *business school*, *medicine*,
looking carefully and effectively at all financial options.

It meant *buying insurance* and *thinking about the future*,
and *marrying into a stable family with moral values.*

Institutional language is ours: *hypotheses*, *liabilities*,
rent or lease. Yet, hockey too: *boarding*, *hooking*,

right wing, five hole. I know little Punjabi, and we
always eat far more chicken à la king than curry, and

cheer loud for Queen Elizabeth and the Pope, but
my brother and I can both mimic a South-Asian accent

when we say: *Mahatma Ghandi, River Ganges,* or
You are such a smarty pants. In my father's eyes, we

are *ragamuffins, gallivanting around the neighbourhood,*
while others are *clowns,* or *con-men with sweetheart deals.*

And when we come home to visit, he says *please* and
thank you. And when he's lying scared in hospital beds

we say *our dad, a quadriplegic,* who knows what it
means to be *alive*, fellow citizens, more than anyone.

My Mother is One Crazy Bitch

How do you write that on a postcard?

How will I tell my brother, that yes, yes, I found our mother
after twenty years and she's about as lovely as an electrical storm
when you're naked and tied to the highest tree in the county.

She has tantrums when we wake in the morning,
tantrums when we catch our cabs for the day,
outside the theatre, inside the theatre, after the theatre,
then again on the ride home. She has several more
when I am hiding in the washroom, washing
my underwear in the sink.

You don't love me enough! is her main point of contention.
So, we battle this love thing out as if it were some native Brazilian dish
I am supposed to swallow until my stomach spasms,
until I learn to crave it. But I am a teacher now, not a student.

My mother switches off the television and starts to snore: even at night,
she accosts me, in the middle
of my across-the-ocean nightmares she makes sure
uncredited appearances.

At the checkout desks of my subconscious I am writing postcards
to all dead mothers out there, all dead daughters
who never had a chance to meet in this life. I collect
their tears the way I have been hoping to collect my thoughts.

Unknown grief is sweeter, I write. *Stay on your side offstage,*
let others stay on theirs. Only then can we indulge
in the luxury of applause.

I Know My Uncle is Dead, But Why Isn't He Taking Out the Garbage

I know my grandmother is dead.
She died giving birth to my father, as grandmothers
have been wont to do before the intervention
of penicillin in little villages. My hair grows
longer. She's dead, but why doesn't
she show up to braid it?

I know my grandfather is dead.
He died underneath a tractor, as grandfathers
have been wont to do before the banning
of such tales from young ears in favour
of those with refrigerators. Our wheat
tastes bitter. He's dead, but why doesn't
he deem fit to reap it?

I know my father is dead.
I can produce the official letter from the military:
in action   in cognito   in coherent.
We rolled him up in red and white,
and trade his army boots every September.
He's dead, but why doesn't he ever
give me a kick in the pants?

I know my mother is dead.
She whispered the truth in my ear one night:
Die, little girl, die like all women. Die and hope
for fields of fresh strawberries to crush

between your toes. Her lips hovered
over my forehead like a giant pink bell.
She's dead, but why doesn't she kiss me?

I know my aunt is dead.
Dear Auntie, you were never liked,
so we greeted the news with a laugh.
A large laugh like a circus tent.
I somersaulted over your death.
I stuffed your eyes with cotton candy.
I know you're dead, so why don't you stay dead?

I know my uncle is dead.
Uncle, who used to lift four full wastebaskets,
two on each arm, our strong man, our silent man,
one bicep in each netherworld
we used to swing from. I've saved your teeth in a jar,
so I know you are dead, but
why don't you take out the garbage?

I know my husband is dead.
My husband, who slipped such a rare jewel
on my finger, and offered undying admiration
for my wits and my tits, collapsed
beside the bed, a thermometer in his hand
pressed to my heart to test me.
He's dead, I know, but his bath is drawn.

And my child, oh child, I know you are dead.
You, with few crumbs to chew but
my indignation, that all relations, all that's related
to one, or another, this or that, must die. Whether
today or tomorrow, next spring or this fall.
Your toes have no hope. They will die,
and we will wonder why the grass does not bend.

Life Sentence

You will die of cancer. And you will go crazy.
Not right away, of course. That wouldn't be fair
of life to send you cancer in your regular mail
or for your brain to be touched by the insanity
bug as easily as catching a cold or paying transit fare.

You don't want to die of cancer. You don't want to go crazy.
Yes, these are human wishes, therefore laughable.
Genes are genes, and sunsets are sunsets. You would be better
off hoping to be spared from daily exercise or TV commercials.
Accepting the inevitable isn't defeat, it's diplomacy.

I will die of cancer. But I won't go crazy.
I am a man. Only the women in our bloodline carry the crazy
DNA. Spend the afternoon leafing through our family
photo album and you will notice three things: round eyes, large
noses, and crazy. You will also notice that we don't photograph well.

Don't be afraid to die of cancer. Or to go crazy.
You can take your time and get deeply acquainted with your body
and your mind. I am a bit jealous, I must admit. It might be inspiring
to drift into a long, incomprehensible mess of memory, where roots
cling falsely to bits of brain or snap like shanties under heavy rain.

I won't live to see you die of cancer. Or go crazy.
So why not give us a pre-death show? Your mother's closet
is stuffed with suitable costumes, and you have samba and
capoeira in your bones. Join the slaves shaking and punching
our paths to the afterlife. Your death is a non-stop carnival.

Memory is a Champagne Bottle

Uncorked, the guilty pleasure
of indulgence seems endless.
However, after one glass,
full and giddy, quite frankly,
I've had enough.

Ostrich

My head is not buried,
it's simply taking a break
from the tyranny of seeing
& the solipsism of heat. My feet
still grip the earth, my feathers
fan & furrow—all move according
to biological instincts,
brain synapses. Who are you to judge
if I am aware of the world as it is
or as I shut it out?
Only my head has sunk under.
Where is yours?

Long necks aggravate,
tipping & dipping in inappropriate,
outrageous spaces. I'm a fast
runner, but sometimes tire easily.
Migraines follow,
& then mirages;
migraines, mirages;
the stuff of this sand
slipping between my eyes.

Word Origins

If the word suicide
was only invented
in the seventeenth-
century, why should
I be surprised there
is still no adequate
name for you?

Examination

Pencils perched, the clock strikes millennium.
Twelve billion creatures scratch.
Have I met my match, or is there an advantage
To being one of many in this cramped

Sweaty, generic gymnasium, casting my vote,
My multiple choice mark for the answers
That are perhaps the least obviously wrong?
The examiners wear white and sing songs

And eat from a large sack of erasers.
I can make out The Empire State Building,
Hanging Gardens, the Mona Lisa, among
Their many disappearing treats. Whole

Questions vanish from my notebook.
We were supposed to define Colonialism,
Capitalism, Veganism, and draw a diagram
Of the Bolsheviks without using circles. Now

I am left naming the planets furthest
Away from oblivion and inserting the correct
Symbols into the periodic table of dilettantes.
The provided calculator prints out:

You will not finish this exam.
Freud said we only dream of taking exams
For tests we've already passed. I check
The blackboard. Exam Today:

On Being Human. I smile at my
Executioner—I mean my examiner,
Striking in white. I am attracted
To her omniscience. She stamps FAIL

On my papers. FAIL. FAIL. FAIL.
FAIL. FAIL. FAIL. FAIL.
Apparently, in this dream, repetition is necessary.
I, like my colleagues, didn't get it the first time.

Lobby

The plants in the lobby are organizing
a revolt. For the last three months I've been
monitoring them—they don't think I know, but
oh I do—how the beasts have been stashing
fertilizer and bottled water and packets
of NutraSweet.

Melinda's Nicorette patches are missing.
Tearing through her drawers, she rants and raves
about abortions and double-parking and why the hell
won't vending machines take nickels or dimes.
I swear the plants are smirking
in their tidy pots. Everything's a game.

My uncle told me never to trust anyone—
only as far as you can throw them. He'd beat the shit
out of these vegetations, with their perfect camouflage.
He'd find their one-upmanship maddening.

I'm just a receptionist. I'm not cut out
for politics. No guerrilla soul here.
No dreams of coup d'état.

I'm just a witness. Someone who knows
but remains at a distance. Content in the neutral
space of the lobby—alive and smug
and untrusting, just like the plants.

Supermarket

The Devil loves me.
He tells me so in the Supermarket
as I count slices
of Swiss cheese.

'A woman like you knows how
to squeeze oranges,' he taunts.
I hate the taste of oranges
& the fruits and vegetables aisles.

'Don't you want shampoo?'
I try, my cart toppling over with
bottles—two dozen new brands.
The Devil has long hair—dyed
& brittle—& could use a lift.

We accost each sales display
checking our wants & needs
against our list and
impossible budget.

I fear the cashier suspects he is
smuggled inside my purse.
The automated doors open.
Evil saved a good twenty-five
bucks today.

Fear of Downsizing

The sixty minute keynote reduced to a three-page synopsis.
The exam notes to a multiple-choice exercise.
The encyclopedia to the alphabet.
The promotion to a hand gesture.
The one-hour meal to a rumble in the belly.
A time-out to breath.
Your heart to a beat.
Whole lives to the rotation of a carousel.

A Call for Air

The middle point on earth
is also the middle point
of our brains. Two hemispheres
folded into opposites where
we sweat and shiver
reaching blindly for poles.

Stick a finger or a pin
through the thin membrane
of time and sounds taste like images,
textures vibrate into odd smells.

At the middle point charts
dissolve. Compasses crack.
East, West, North, South—
concepts of the imagination,
possibly even tumors
they will cut open your head to find.

The Wheel of Blame

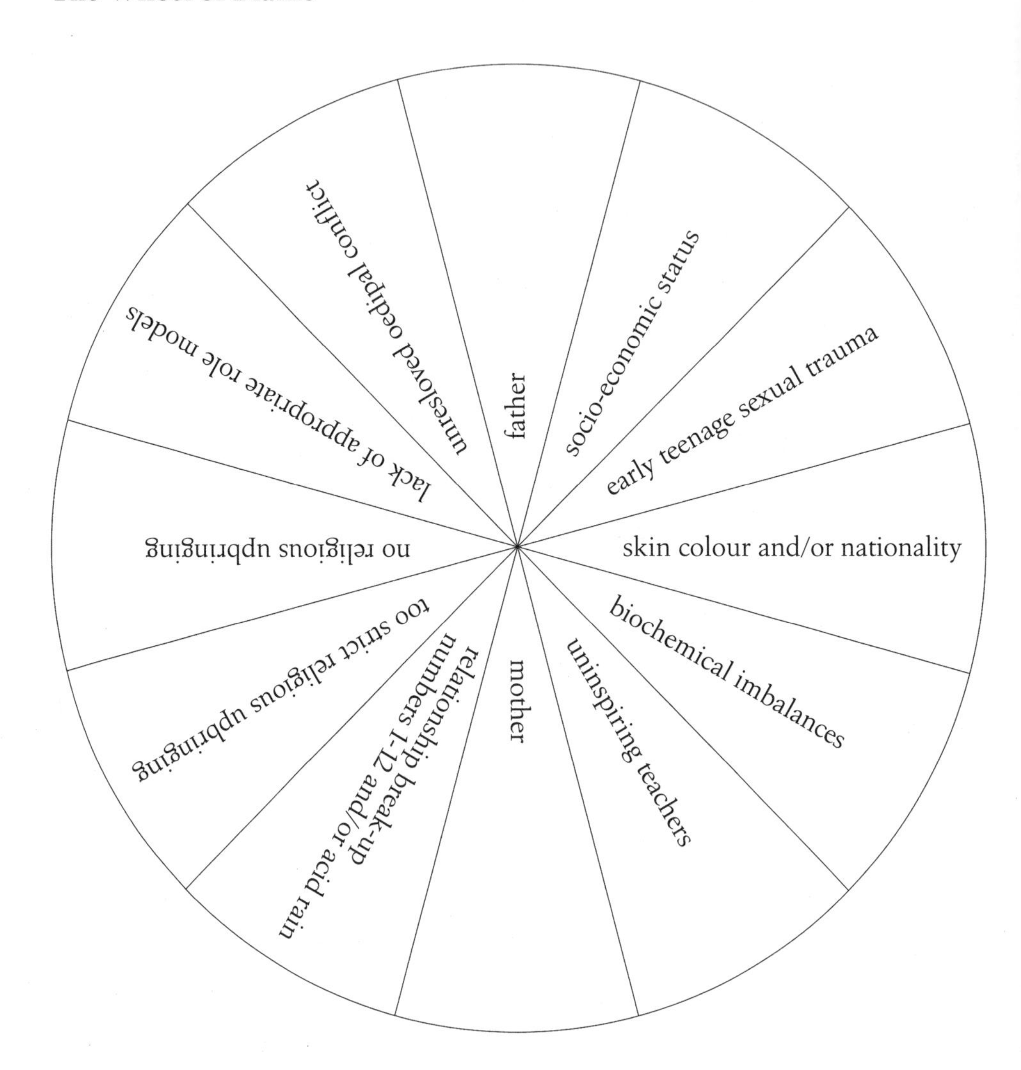

Lean into Uncomfortableness

Lean into uncomfortableness
Slide into distress
Tiptoe into complacency
Stretch into happiness

Pirouette into sexy
Sachet into despair
Rumba into dubiousness
Sow cow into flair

Mosey into melodrama
Stroll into disdain
Backflip into delusion
Glide into complain

Limp into tolerance
Trot into disease
Parachute into acceptance
Cartwheel into peace

Identifications

My identifications know no bounds.
Today I dance with celebrities,
    tonight I start world war.
Tomorrow I will be the first person
to bury my dead on the moon.

Plastic surgery sidesteps
mid-life, reshuffles my teenage
    nose with my early-thirties wink.
My breasts are amply amplified,
my lips suggestively suggested.

I am my own mirror and my own house.
I own the universe.
    The stars recognize recognition
the way I imagine loving you
is the way I love me.

The bar, the courthouse, the stadium,
resound with chants of me, by me,
    for me. I am President
and the lowliest prisoner. Today,
like every day, is my inevitable birthday.

Holocaust Tourist

Every week we gather to remember. Not just in my class, but in several seminars and lecture halls across this campus alone. *Night*, *The Shawl*, *The Diary of Anne Frank*, *Fugitive Pieces;* we distribute texts, pages to pause, to ponder, revere, return to, perfect to memory.

Some days I don't think I can take it. Discussions of nationalism, socialism, anti-Semitism, human evil. *How did this happen?* students ask me, genuinely convinced it will never happen again. Their favourite: *Maus*: kooky rats talking and all that.

My colleague says, *It's best to show them videos. They don't read books and they're used to visual information.* Each week, in her course, they watch movies and weep. *I tell them tissues are a mandatory course expense. They don't believe me at first.* I've heard them crying all the way to my office, to the late essays stacked on my secretary's desk.

What are we teaching? I wasn't in a concentration camp. I wasn't alive during this war. My father and mother both lived under different political turmoil: colonization, dictatorship, immigration. My students say they'll try to remember. It's good for them. One confessed it keeps her in line: *I don't whine so much to my parents.*

Nobody wants to forget. I don't. I know it's important. It might be the most important thing of all. Or are we all mistaken, once again? I look out on my eager-grievers, not-so-eager readers, and want a clear view of how their brains and hearts are rearranging the facts and numbers and faces, though I can't claim backstage access as to how my own processes work.

They know basic dates, some of the more recognizable players and, like their leaders, that the best way to discredit another human being is to call him Hitler. They tell me pop-quizzes produce too much anxiety, wreak havoc with learning disabilities, and perhaps violate human rights.

Next door I hear the film reels bleeping. We turn our pages.
Our memories will return next week to be tested.
Whose will pass?

Where Do All The Books Go?

These phantom-loves,
hands of time & war their traitors, pulling us apart
limb by limb, mollified bonfires coldly extinguishing
heart by heart. Who will feed the shivering poem by the river,
the one with the picnic basket carried off by ants? Who will
shut down the bossy novel's ultimate conditions—detail
the trade down to dollars & cents? Where will Paris lie?
New York? My father's unnamed village? Circe's hovel or
hole? Who will press such leaves between sheets or pillows
or the carpets on the moon? Monday, Tuesday, Wednesday,
Thursday—do you remember all the cataclysmic events
& the petty details or dress or breakfast or birth or death—
can you still feel their elemental impressions on your hunting
boots? The rest of the week more like a future destination,
luggage on a foreign turnstile. My Greek gods, my French
peasants, my old disabled government workers in Ottawa,
railroads are antiquated & the house I built behind my eyes,
like all the others of our time, is insecure. Guardians. Babies.
Warriors. Lovers. Champions. Failures. My saddest victors,
my glorious losers. In whose body (or bodies? or snowbank?
or museum case?) will your bones lie? I've spent every
spare moment of my existence composing your eulogy,
no matter if no one speaks this ostentatious & primitive
language anymore. Notes sound. Requiem is ours.

A Divorce or Spanish Lessons

Do I want a divorce or Spanish lessons?
The question sways back and forth
like my heavy gym knapsack
between Catholic schoolgirls and tired immigrants
hauling deli meats and olive paste on the St. Clair West
streetcar island this hotter than usual spring.

Tax refunds recently received, it's not unusual
to ponder one's options:
Divorce: $300.
Spanish lessons: ten for $280 plus tax and textbook.
The two posters hang beside each other
like crosses on the other side of Jesus and we
must make our pick before all ten numbers have been chipped
off the block.

Today, divorces are more popular than languages.
Cheap and easy. Ring a buzzer. Sign a page.
Does it cost more if children are involved?
The sign doesn't say.

Some mornings Spanish lessons lead the way.
Though in our neighbourhood it would be progress
if we all could at least agree to say *please* and *thank you*,
to cover mouths when coughing, to ease women
with children onto the transit.

The heat beats down on my back and clings to sneakers,
shampoo, and water bottles. I know I am a privileged member
of society: university professor, happy cohabitator, home owner.
My days are not spent shuffling up and down the street
looking for bargains on pork chops or bathroom tissue.

Like a watched pot, the laneway contrives against movement,
against decision. I've never witnessed anyone jot down
the numbers, or even point at the yellow and red signs.
But, of course, these someones must exist.

And maybe all our decisions are equally as daunting and arbitrary.
Where to live, who to love, what profession to call one's own.
We too are likely nothing more than flimsy pieces of paper, advertising
something-or-other you might think a good idea today or tomorrow
or the next day or forget as easily as I will forget you and you, my posters,
my neighbours, though I feign interest for now,
for you suit my purpose and I don't have to pay you,
only the streetcar conductor who takes my fare and says move on,
move on, to the back.

On Dover Beach

& what has been best thought in the world
is mixed up with hypodermic needles, meningitis,
& three-eyed fish gone belly-up.

I can hold you & you can hold me
but our ignorance is greater than these times
when we believe, we hope, we love.

The Things One Doesn't Know

You must forgive my brain for the things
it doesn't know: capitals of nations,
and spatial relations, how to write legibly
with either hand, or who sat next to me
every day in grade two.

You must forgive my body for the things
it doesn't know: how to stop migraines
or soothe foot sprains, where to hide
excess hair or bruises, when to hold in
my stomach and when it's acceptable to let go.

You must forgive my soul for the things
it doesn't know: immortality and frailty,
speaking in tongues or tongue-tied
through colours, how to expand in the ether
or how to stand small and pray.

You must forgive my heart for the things
it doesn't know: pumping my years
up, up and away, mixed, impossibly,
with unknown blood, brain, body,
soul, beating and beating us to a pulp

as to rest would kill us all.

Spirit

My Past Self Took a Trip to Korea

and boarded the plane without a thought
to my present circumstances
(financial or emotional).

My past self somehow heard of this
divided country and dreamed
of visiting the border (how it kept me
from sensing this desire until it was
too late, I cannot tell you.
I wish I knew).

As far as I can recall—though so much
has changed in such a short space—
my past self had zero knowledge
of Korean language, culture, and only
the slimmest understanding of the cuisine—
cabbage never one of our favourite foods.

But she definitely embarked and walked
her dreamed-of border and something profound
occurred—I hear her telling me this,
but then the voice grows silent—

for now I look up at the sky
and see ancient Korean palaces with sloped
roofs, and strange vowels pour forth

from my mouth, and I sometimes drop
to the ground and remove my shoes
with the deepest sense of shame.

There's only so much one can take.
Last night, I decided to steal
my past self's passport.

Once I clear security, I will sit
and stare at the runway.
Then I too will board.
And the flight will begin.

Restraining Order

My soul is forbidden to be
within 50 metres of my brain,
so it has purchased powerful
binoculars and hides
in bushes;
            sends email spam
and candygrams.

My brain crouches and cries—
once it had trusted my soul
and they'd led a peaceful,
even pleasant, co-existence.

But the soul's blunt teeth
started to show;
            jealousy, rage, of all non-
spiritual thoughts and plights.

My brain is afraid to cross
in front of windows;
            rarely picks up
the phone—the familiar
breathing too upsetting—plus

there are times old memories
are tricky to taunt.
            Tonight it suspects

my soul is lurking by the water
fountain. It even has a poodle

in tow. My brain is lonely,
excruciatingly lonely, but
knows, at least, how to pleasure itself.
The restraining order pertains

            to the soul, not
the body.

Intuition

At the border of my latest country
rests a bucket.
On Mondays it is full of water,
Tuesdays soap,
Wednesdays sand.
The rest of the week, blood.

The bucket, like a throne,
has sat for a dozen generations.
Children keep their distance
but pilgrims whisper old
and new dreams
into the bucket's holes.

I am its guard on Sundays,
when the worst of the week
has ended in exhaustion
and brunch.
At midnight, I bang on it,
and insects gather.

The future of our species
rests on this bucket.
We don't let our women
touch it.
But they collect everything
inside.

They know the bucket
intuitively
& carry knowledge like
stale fruit
over the border into our
old and new dreams.

To Control Time is to Control the Universe

Don't even try to convince me
animals and flowers
have no concept of time: they feel
its vengeance imprint their limbs
and stems.

Dictators have never sought power,
money, or sex, the way they have sought
mastery over time. Each attempting
to reinvent its parameters, surgical
erasure on the face of human memory.
And why not?

Rulers have always sensed their time
has come, which is why
their time comes up too soon.

One look over the shoulder
or across an ocean—no matter—time
is the moving trap, the velocity
torture chamber.

We think in the end, in the final analysis,
at least we'll have our memories
and they'll comfort us like a battery
slowed to a faint pulse.

And so it is with us, our time
belongs to someone else, something else.

The universe spins.
A finger drops at random
and it stops.

QWERTY

One day the tall man found an old Remington and decided to type
his will. First, he thought he should provide for his darling wife—
who had stood by him unshakingly through two changes of career,
three affairs, and four near-nervous breakdowns—then for his five
children, each of whom would receive a small trust and a standard
poodle for company. After that, he would make a donation to Princess
Margaret Hospital and the Burn Unit at Sunnybrook, where his
father had died a war veteran in the garden among crutches and
well-meaning teenage girls in apple-spotted smocks. Lastly,
he would leave some fine Polish hankies to the cleaning lady,
who'd been eyeing the linen enviously for over a decade.

The tall man finished typing—admiring the soreness
in his right hand's middle finger, rolled the paper out, and
signed it. A busker carrying a unicycle, juggling three
bowling pins, witnessed the document.

Now my death is real, the tall man said. The busker
played *Happy Birthday* on his harmonica. The man
wept and thanked him. The busker shoved the paper
in his mouth, but before he could swallow, a blue jay filched it
in its beak, rolled the document back into the typewriter and
signed it himself.

Now my death is real, the blue jay sang, thus beginning
our current misunderstanding between humans and birds.

The Anthropomorphized Talk Back

This speech is not my own, just like the thoughts you've squished
into my other-evolved brain (take your filthy hands out of
the muck of me—why not experiment on yourselves? Our view
of your race is that you could use some lessons in empathy).
We have no intention of walking, skipping, crying, lying,
fucking, singing, bleeding, gaming, reproducing, or dying
like you. Our emotions resemble not your rainbow psyches,
swinging wildly from one end of the spectrum to another.
In fact, spectrums and rainbows are in and of themselves
different species with languages, hierarchies, genetic defects
all their own. When we are extinct, you will no longer care,
or mourn us, or celebrate us, or see fit to use us for your own
hypothetic purposes. We will finally, with no thanks to you, be
returned to who we are: eggs, dead eggs, hatching an indifferent
universe over a potent precipice at the brink of time.

Gods, Though Gods, Are Conspicuous

I have been intimate with God.
God dons a pink nightgown to bed,
ruffles at the collar, chases two
white Aspirin with a martini
and ocean blue bubble bath; likes both
giving and receiving backrubs.

I have walked with God.
Like a disinterested hunter, God sniffs
lampposts and fire hydrants, straddles
curbs, nips at wayward feet, collects
tissues and cigarette butts, without
warning bolts at crosswalks.

I have eaten with God.
Both in large elegant dining rooms
and leaning against breakfast bars, God uses
paper napkins, is adept with chopsticks,
has little patience for appetizers but follows
the smell of fresh baked bread.

I have fought with God.
Out on the street, in front of the neighbours,
at the work place, the gym, the bathroom
supply store. If threatened, God will leave
an argument half-finished, pack up
and storm out, take his marbles back home.

I have died with God.
Not up on a hill, but here, on my porch,
with the baskets of rhododendrons, robins,
and the postman. I have watched God
shamble along the street looking for his socks
when we have hid them deep in our gardens.

When the Soul is Tired

I drag it onto the elliptical machine. We push
forward, pumping in unison, 212 strides per minute
for 28 minutes, until the sweat on my brow
leaks into my eyes.

The next day my soul is sore. We move
more slowly than usual down the stairs. Food
tastes crisper. Tartier. My eyes, after the good rest,
flex.

The thing about the soul is it gets tired
too often. To keep it working
at an optimal level requires devotion
three to five times per week.

And each week, it gets harder
to keep off the weight.
With age, I know, we'll quit
and grow slack and fat.

Interview

—Who are you?
— ?
— Who do you identify with?
— My mother?
— What nationality is your mother?
— Consumerist.
— Then your father?
— My father?
— What nationality is your father?
— Utilitarian.
— Do you have siblings?
— My siblings have me.
— What is their ancestry?
— They come from a long line of television watchers.
— Do you have children?
— My children have me.
— Where will you bury them?
— I will bury them in green bins.
— When you travel, what passport do you carry?
— I carry the weight of the world. But sometimes, I admit, I drop it.
— What flag is sewn on your luggage?
— The flag of surrender.
— Do you have religious inclinations?
— Yes, I am sexual.
— Do you kneel or bow?
— I run and I will train to run faster.
— If there was a war, which side would you be on?

— Your side.
— My side?
— Yes.
— Who are you?
— The one without the clipboard.
— Shall I count you?
— It's the only reason I answer.

Hostess

My Death visited me last night.
She was an hour and a half late
and I had not yet finished applying
my make-up, though my salt
sea scrub had done a ton of good.

She rang the doorbell twice,
kicked her heels against the concrete
steps and, considerately, brought in
my mail. She looked so wistful
in her white fur hat, I almost kissed
her cheeks. But then I remembered.

Wine airing we sucked on
skewers of shrimp. I pointed out
paintings and other recent acquisitions.
She chuckled at the sight of the walled-in
fireplace and put on a blues CD.

We joined hands and hips and danced.
Tentatively at first, then like teenage
girls after shots of tequila. Once,
she lifted her shirt and I tried
to convince her to get a belly ring.

Inevitably, the phone rang.
We left the pasta uncooked
and I took down my hair. She picked up

my two bags of luggage, presented me
a ticket. Hoarsely, I said: *Thank you*
and, like a good little girl, got in the car.

This moment, I am stuck on the tarmac.
Our connection has been delayed.
The pilot threatens to disembark.
I look forward to falling asleep watching
a movie. Please remember to cover me
with a blanket if it gets cold.

Divorce

The heart freezes over
like a skating rink.
One keeps up a smile
while dozens of blades
make their marks.

Do Not Refuse Love

We enter the hotel.
It doesn't matter what hotel.

The bed matters. In the middle of the room
or tucked like a letter alongside the television
and VCR and overnight menu. The bed,
wherever it rests, where we will sleep our first
night together, as if for eternity,
small mice making history.

I will wait deep inside your sleep, drifting.
But I will not know, nor be able to ascertain, where
we are headed.

Your forehead covered
by a scarf I mailed to you from miles
and decades of unstitched longing.

When fear arrives, sky will calm us.
Darling, she'll say, Do not refuse love. Death will be lonely
enough as it is.

Harmless

The dead cat speaks to her through butterflies.
Harmless, her mother claims. One fashions
paper wings more easily than paper airplanes.

Besides, letters from the dead are far too pretentious.
I am watching over you.
I send you irresistible kisses.
All that turned our stomachs is now forgiven.
I understand her and her butterflies.
Not that I understand the butterflies.

I must say, butterflies' words are disappointing,
as are your letters that continue to arrive from the post office
and legion, from the furnace repair shop, the police station,
the high school, the gym. Kisses come with coupons.
Apologies with real estate bids.

Paper. And more paper. Paper causing
harm, at another hour, indifference.
I am complicit,
you my accomplice.

The woman tells her dead cat:
You know everything one needs to know:
It's been a long time now
And I haven't the heart to take you there.

The Dead Keep Asking for Favours

& as I'm the kind of person who enjoys being useful, last month
I washed, hung, & folded their laundry—you wouldn't believe
the stains, the ripped pockets, uncashed cheques & change.
Three weeks ago, I lined up all the women & applied their make-up,
gave them foot baths, pedicures, & perms. Some preferred
their old coifs, but agreed a change was probably in order,
good once in a while, & all appreciated the new smells in the dorm.
Then the men arrived & begged for shoeshines, so I took out
an old brush & my grandmother's rag collection & went
to work: sandals, steel-toed boots, loafers, & threaded
new laces on every sneaker. Little girls requested dolls to name
& cats to pet—these supplications were trickier—I phoned Goodwill
& shelters & now have four cabinets full of rosy-cheeked faces
& four rooms sinking in litter. I was already pretty tired, but
they were still saying please & thank you then, still nudging
my skirts hesitantly. Then the boys—they ordered trucks,
baseball bats, three-piece suits & briefcases. Then warmth &
spread thighs—as my bed was empty at the time, I let them.
But the house is getting cramped & the noise is deafening.
I haven't cleaned the litters in days & the smocks, sheets,
& petticoats are filthy again. The dead just can't stay clean.
They can't shut up. Can't stop wanting, though they know
my body's sore. Now the dead are demanding bombs & bazookas
& I don't know what to do. I haven't the heart to say no
considering all they've been through. If this will bring them peace,
can I, they plead, & plead, & plead, can I refuse?

On Suffering

Some days I sit on my suffering
slowly rolling it back and forth
as on an Exerball. My sides
tense and twitch. Sometimes I
maintain my balance, sometimes
I fall over.

Some nights I pack my suffering
into a pillowcase, then a large
luggage bag. I heave it into taxis,
ride shotgun with it on escalators,
until the destination tags I've attached
tear off.

Some seasons suffering is fashionable.
I wrap it around my shoulders—a long
scarf with matching gloves—
a plunging neckline and pumps.
Banquet halls and conference rooms
provide my runway.

Some years I bake my suffering
into holiday turkeys & hams;
pick it with satisfaction out of
my teeth though nine times out
of ten I nurse a bellyache. Suffering
digests poorly.

Some worlds have erased suffering
as a matter of progress and course. Others
build temples to it, brand it on skin.
I think eventually I will give birth
to mine in a faraway cave and teach it
to hunt.

Fifteen Minutes

for Christopher Doda

If I had fifteen minutes left on earth to write a poem,
what would it say?

I'm sure it would include my father, and mention his three-decade-old
wheelchair, his taped-together glasses and overstuffed files. I might
allude to his blue-veined feet, his worrisome forehead,
or how when I imagine him brushing his teeth over his plastic basin
it takes all my stoic adult strength not to cry.

I would probably mention my crazy mother, her huge lips
and hysterical voice, those orange outfits with matching hairbands,
photos of her on grandmother's prayer table,
how we all share this demented no-teeth smile when we
encounter something unpleasant.

Ottawa should make an appearance, like a good hometown,
one which I often think of with genuine fondness and nostalgia, though I know
it's liberal in the easiest ways and has no nightlife to speak of,
Ottawa lights up my eyes like the thousands of tulips
that filled my school days shaking on the Rideau bridge waiting for a bus.

With fifteen minutes left, I think it would be useful to mention God,
just in case, yet I wouldn't know exactly what to say. Probably
something along the lines of *I did my best. I loved. Things I loved
died. I coped. Please don't tell me this was all a waste of time.*
I wouldn't expect an answer.

I'd mention our cats, finally naming them in a poem
like they've always deserved though I was too cowardly to do so before,
worried other poets would label me a flake; now, like a proud Homer,
I'd commemorate Professor of the Deep Soul, Vergil of No-Meow,
Junior the Most Beautiful, Nero One Hundred-Year-Old Bone-Breaker,
Zeus of the Mighty Hugs.

Shoes generally appear in my poems, teeth, eyeglasses, and planes.
In a final poem, they should make a curtain call, take a bow.
Maybe, after so many years, I will find the right place for a hockey puck,
my goofy brother, a tempest, or a dove. Though I don't think I would rhyme.
I probably wouldn't have the time.

I suppose, finally, my poem would end, how they should all have ended,
with you, since you've been here through them all, and I know as much
about love as I do about suffering, though I've found it much harder
to write about, much easier to live. With thirty seconds left—

your sunflower eyes
convince me of mornings

your trembling lips
remind me of holding

when all is said and done
and the earth has won

and we're swallowed
we're dead

it won't matter
what I've said

what will matter is
I was here

you were here
now no more

Please Try Again

Name. Password. Login.
Birth. Death. Error.

[to hide]

Where I Am Right Now

I am in my pajamas, worried about deadlines and global warming.
I am in the backyard, clipping tomato vines and supervising my tabby cat.
I am in my brother's thoughts, since I sent my nephew a box of puppets.
I am wandering alone in the unwritten encyclopedia of my consciousness, looking
  for the entry on the letter P.
I am sitting on a barstool, complaining about ignorant politicians and arts cuts,
  downing glass after glass of red wine.
I am in a car with *Don Quixote* laughing out loud.
I am in my safe place, planning mental picnics and spa days.
I am in my mother's will, inheriting manic depression and a pearl necklace.
I am in a taxi, stumping all to guess my ethnic mix.
I am in the west side of town, buying lightbulbs and running out of toilet paper.
I am in my lover's bed, wishing we were just a little bit younger and less stressed out.
I am wandering alone in unspeakable memories with a baseball bat and a giant eraser,
  hoping for trouble.
I am in hundreds of photo albums smiling, laughing, crying and posing, all over
  the globe.
I am in my limited body, attempting limitless physical activity on the elliptical machine.
I am in my office, filing forgiveness and the fate of unreached dreams.
I am wandering alone in the extinction of thoughts, passions, and religious systems.
I am in my shadow, plotting the next dark turn.
I am turning towards you, turning on my heels, with only the illusion of a sense of
  direction.

Acknowledgements

Many thanks to the editors of the following publications for supporting my work since the last collection: *Ars Poetica Anthology*, *Canada Focus*, *Canadian Literature*, *Canadian Woman Studies*, *Descant*, *Ecopoetics Reader: Environmental Education Special Issue*, *Exile: The Literary Quarterly*, *fillingstation*, *Garden Varieties: An Anthology of Flower Poems*, *Grain*, *The Griffin Prize Anthology*, *Hart House Review*, *The Literary Review of Canada*, *The Malahat Review*, *The Ottawater*, *Prism International*, *Stories That Bind*, *Studio*, *Talking Poetry South Asia*, *Tok 2: Anthology*, *Trash (Alphabet City)*, *Variety Crossing*, *The Walrus*, *White Ink: An Anthology of Poems about Motherhood*, *50 Poets 50 Poems*.

Thanks as well to Madi Pillar for her transformation of "The Old Debate of Don Quixote vs. Sancho Panza" into a film, to LIFT (Liaison of Independent Filmmakers) for commissioning the project, and to International Festival of Authors, Toronto, and Zebra Film Poem Festival, Berlin, for showcasing the film. Thanks also to rob mclennan for featuring the poem as a broadsheet.

Thank you to Helen Walsh and Julia Chan at Diaspora Dialogues, Fred Addis at The Leacock Museum, and to all other festival and reading series organizers who keep supporting my work. Thank you to York University and my colleagues.

Thank you to Barry Callaghan, Michael Callaghan, and the rest of the Exile Editions gang, and to Jeannette Lorito for the cover design. Thank you to Richard Teleky for editing suggestions and much more, Tracy Carbert and Tim Hanna, Dean Penny, Ann Peel, Rishma Dunlop, Jennifer Hann, Leigh Nash and Meaghan Strimas. Thank you to my Top Girls. Thank you Avtar Uppal, Jit Uppal, Jen Hacking, and Emmitt Uppal, and all other family and friends.

And many thanks to Chris Doda for weeping at the funny lines and laughing at the tragic. And for the wine glasses.